The Poetry of Algernon Charles Swinburne

VOLUME IV – SONGS OF TWO NATIONS

Algernon Charles Swinburne was born on April 5th, 1837, in London, into a wealthy Northumbrian family. He was educated at Eton and at Balliol College, Oxford, but did not complete a degree.

In 1860 Swinburne published two verse dramas but achieved his first literary success in 1865 with Atalanta in Calydon, written in the form of classical Greek tragedy. The following year "Poems and Ballads" brought him instant notoriety. He was now identified with "indecent" themes and the precept of art for art's sake.

Although he produced much after this success in general his popularity and critical reputation declined. The most important qualities of Swinburne's work are an intense lyricism, his intricately extended and evocative imagery, metrical virtuosity, rich use of assonance and alliteration, and bold, complex rhythms.

Swinburne's physical appearance was small, frail, and plagued by several other oddities of physique and temperament. Throughout the 1860s and 1870s he drank excessively and was prone to accidents that often left him bruised, bloody, or unconscious. Until his forties he suffered intermittent physical collapses that necessitated removal to his parents' home while he recovered.

Throughout his career Swinburne also published literary criticism of great worth. His deep knowledge of world literatures contributed to a critical style rich in quotation, allusion, and comparison. He is particularly noted for discerning studies of Elizabethan dramatists and of many English and French poets and novelists. As well he was a noted essayist and wrote two novels.

In 1879, Swinburne's friend and literary agent, Theodore Watts-Dunton, intervened during a time when Swinburne was dangerously ill. Watts-Dunton isolated Swinburne at a suburban home in Putney and gradually weaned him from alcohol, former companions and many other habits as well.

Much of his poetry in this period may be inferior but some individual poems are exceptional; "By the North Sea," "Evening on the Broads," "A Nympholept," "The Lake of Gaube," and "Neap-Tide."

Swinburne lived another thirty years with Watts-Dunton. He denied Swinburne's friends access to him, controlled the poet's money, and restricted his activities. It is often quoted that 'he saved the man but killed the poet'.

Swinburne died on April 10th, 1909 at the age of seventy-two.

Index of Contents
A SONG OF ITALY
ODE ON THE PROCLAMATION OF THE FRENCH REPUBLIC
DIRAE

I - A DEAD KING
II - A YEAR AFTER
III - PETER'S PENCE FROM PERUGIA
IV - PAPAL ALLOCUTION
V - THE BURDEN OF AUSTRIA. 1866
VI - LOCUSTA
VII - CELAENO
VIII - A CHOICE
IX - THE AUGURS
X - A COUNSEL
XI - THE MODERATES
XII - INTERCESSION
XIII - THE SAVIOUR OF SOCIETY
XIV - MENTANA: SECOND ANNIVERSARY
XV - MENTANA: THIRD ANNIVERSARY
XVI - THE DESCENT INTO HELL
XVII - APOLOGIA
ALGERBON CHARLES SWINBURNE – A SHORT BIOGRAPHY
ALGERNON CHARLES SWINBURNE – A CONCISE BIBLIOGRAPHY

DIRAE

I saw the double-featured statue stand
Of Memnon or of Janus, half with night
Veiled, and fast bound with iron; half with light
Crowned, holding all men's future in his hand.

And all the old westward face of time grown grey
Was writ with cursing and inscribed for death;
But on the face that met the mornings breath
Fear died of hope as darkness dies of day.

A SONG OF ITALY

Inscribed With All Devotion and Reverence To: JOSEPH MAZZINI

1867

Upon a windy night of stars that fell
At the wind's spoken spell,
Swept with sharp strokes of agonizing light
From the clear gulf of night,
Between the fixed and fallen glories one
Against my vision shone,

More fair and fearful and divine than they
That measure night and day,
And worthier worship; and within mine eyes
The formless folded skies
Took shape and were unfolded like as flowers.
And I beheld the hours
As maidens, and the days as labouring men,
And the soft nights again
As wearied women to their own souls wed,
And ages as the dead.
And over these living, and them that died,
From one to the other side
A lordlier light than comes of earth or air
Made the world's future fair.
A woman like to love in face, but not
A thing of transient lot—
And like to hope, but having hold on truth—
And like to joy or youth,
Save that upon the rock her feet were set—
And like what men forget,
Faith, innocence, high thought, laborious peace—
And yet like none of these,
Being not as these are mortal, but with eyes
That sounded the deep skies
And clove like wings or arrows their clear way
Through night and dawn and day—
So fair a presence over star and sun
Stood, making these as one.
For in the shadow of her shape were all
Darkened and held in thrall,
So mightier rose she past them; and I felt
Whose form, whose likeness knelt
With covered hair and face and clasped her knees;
And knew the first of these
Was Freedom, and the second Italy.
And what sad words said she
For mine own grief I knew not, nor had heart
Therewith to bear my part
And set my songs to sorrow; nor to hear
How tear by sacred tear
Fell from her eyes as flowers or notes that fall
In some slain feaster's hall
Where in mid music and melodious breath
Men singing have seen death.
So fair, so lost, so sweet she knelt; or so
In our lost eyes below
Seemed to us sorrowing; and her speech being said,
Fell, as one who falls dead.

And for a little she too wept, who stood
Above the dust and blood
And thrones and troubles of the world; then spake,
As who bids dead men wake.
"Because the years were heavy on thy head;
Because dead things are dead;
Because thy chosen on hill-side, city and plain
Are shed as drops of rain;
Because all earth was black, all heaven was blind,
And we cast out of mind;
Because men wept, saying Freedom, knowing of thee,
Child, that thou wast not free;
Because wherever blood was not shame was
Where thy pure foot did pass;
Because on Promethean rocks distent
Thee fouler eagles rent;
Because a serpent stains with slime and foam
This that is not thy Rome;
Child of my womb, whose limbs were made in me,
Have I forgotten thee?
In all thy dreams through all these years on wing,
Hast thou dreamed such a thing?
The mortal mother-bird outsoars her nest,
The child outgrows the breast;
But suns as stars shall fall from heaven and cease,
Ere we twain be as these;
Yea, utmost skies forget their utmost sun,
Ere we twain be not one.
My lesser jewels sewn on skirt and hem,
I have no heed of them
Obscured and flawed by sloth or craft or power;
But thou, that wast my flower,
The blossom bound between my brows and worn
In sight of even and morn
From the last ember of the flameless west
To the dawn's baring breast—
I were not Freedom if thou wert not free,
Nor thou wert Italy.
O mystic rose ingrained with blood, impearled
With tears of all the world!
The torpor of their blind brute-ridden trance
Kills England and chills France;
And Spain sobs hard through strangling blood; and snows
Hide the huge eastern woes.
But thou, twin-born with morning, nursed of noon,
And blessed of star and moon!
What shall avail to assail thee any more,
From sacred shore to shore?

Have Time and Love not knelt down at thy feet,
Thy sore, thy soiled, thy sweet,
Fresh from the flints and mire of murderous ways
And dust of travelling days?
Hath Time not kissed them, Love not washed them fair,
And wiped with tears and hair?
Though God forget thee, I will not forget;
Though heaven and earth be set
Against thee, O unconquerable child,
Abused, abased, reviled,
Lift thou not less from no funereal bed
Thine undishonoured head;
Love thou not less, by lips of thine once prest,
This my now barren breast;
Seek thou not less, being well assured thereof,
O child, my latest love.
For now the barren bosom shall bear fruit,
Songs leap from lips long mute,
And with my milk the mouths of nations fed
Again be glad and red
That were worn white with hunger and sorrow and thirst;
And thou, most fair and first,
Thou whose warm hands and sweet live lips I feel
Upon me for a seal,
Thou whose least looks, whose smiles and little sighs,
Whose passionate pure eyes,
Whose dear fair limbs that neither bonds could bruise
Nor hate of men misuse,
Whose flower-like breath and bosom, O my child,
O mine and undefiled,
Fill with such tears as burn like bitter wine
These mother's eyes of mine,
Thrill with huge passions and primeval pains
The fullness of my veins,
O sweetest head seen higher than any stands,
I touch thee with mine hands,
I lay my lips upon thee, O thou most sweet,
To lift thee on thy feet
And with the fire of mine to fill thine eyes;
I say unto thee, Arise."

II

She ceased, and heaven was full of flame and sound,
And earth's old limbs unbound
Shone and waxed warm with fiery dew and seed
Shed through her at this her need:

And highest in heaven, a mother and full of grace,
With no more covered face,
With no more lifted hands and bended knees,
Rose, as from sacred seas
Love, when old time was full of plenteous springs,
That fairest-born of things,
The land that holds the rest in tender thrall
For love's sake in them all,
That binds with words and holds with eyes and hands
All hearts in all men's lands.
So died the dream whence rose the live desire
That here takes form and fire,
A spirit from the splendid grave of sleep
Risen, that ye should not weep,
Should not weep more nor ever, O ye that hear
And ever have held her dear,
Seeing now indeed she weeps not who wept sore,
And sleeps not any more.
Hearken ye towards her, O people, exalt your eyes;
Is this a thing that dies?

III

Italia! by the passion of the pain
That bent and rent thy chain;
Italia! by the breaking of the bands,
The shaking of the lands;
Beloved, O men's mother, O men's queen,
Arise, appear, be seen!
Arise, array thyself in manifold
Queen's raiment of wrought gold;
With girdles of green freedom, and with red
Roses, and white snow shed
Above the flush and frondage of the hills
That all thy deep dawn fills
And all thy clear night veils and warms with wings
Spread till the morning sings;
The rose of resurrection, and the bright
Breast lavish of the light,
The lady lily like the snowy sky
Ere the stars wholly die;
As red as blood, and whiter than a wave,
Flowers grown as from thy grave,
From the green fruitful grass in Maytime hot,
Thy grave, where thou art not.
Gather the grass and weave, in sacred sign
Of the ancient earth divine,

The holy heart of things, the seed of birth,
The mystical warm earth.
O thou her flower of flowers, with treble braid
Be thy sweet head arrayed,
In witness of her mighty motherhood
Who bore thee and found thee good,
Her fairest-born of children, on whose head
Her green and white and red
Are hope and light and life, inviolate
Of any latter fate.
Fly, O our flag, through deep Italian air,
Above the flags that were,
The dusty shreds of shameful battle-flags
Trampled and rent in rags,
As withering woods in autumn's bitterest breath
Yellow, and black as death;
Black as crushed worms that sicken in the sense,
And yellow as pestilence.
Fly, green as summer and red as dawn and white
As the live heart of light,
The blind bright womb of colour unborn, that brings
Forth all fair forms of things,
As freedom all fair forms of nations dyed
In divers-coloured pride.
Fly fleet as wind on every wind that blows
Between her seas and snows,
From Alpine white, from Tuscan green, and where
Vesuvius reddens air.
Fly! and let all men see it, and all kings wail,
And priests wax faint and pale,
And the cold hordes that moan in misty places
And the funereal races
And the sick serfs of lands that wait and wane
See thee and hate thee in vain.
In the clear laughter of all winds and waves,
In the blown grass of graves,
In the long sound of fluctuant boughs of trees,
In the broad breath of seas,
Bid the sound of thy flying folds be heard;
And as a spoken word
Full of that fair god and that merciless
Who rends the Pythoness,
So be the sound and so the fire that saith
She feels her ancient breath
And the old blood move in her immortal veins.

IV

Strange travail and strong pains,
Our mother, hast thou borne these many years
While thy pure blood and tears
Mixed with the Tyrrhene and the Adrian sea;
Light things were said of thee,
As of one buried deep among the dead;
Yea, she hath been, they said,
She was when time was younger, and is not;
The very cerecloths rot
That flutter in the dusty wind of death,
Not moving with her breath;
Far seasons and forgotten years enfold
Her dead corpse old and cold
With many windy winters and pale springs:
She is none of this world's things.
Though her dead head like a live garland wear
The golden-growing hair
That flows over her breast down to her feet,
Dead queens, whose life was sweet
In sight of all men living, have been found
So cold, so clad, so crowned,
With all things faded and with one thing fair,
Their old immortal hair,
When flesh and bone turned dust at touch of day:
And she is dead as they.
So men said sadly, mocking; so the slave,
Whose life was his soul's grave;
So, pale or red with change of fast and feast,
The sanguine-sandalled priest;
So the Austrian, when his fortune came to flood,
And the warm wave was blood;
With wings that widened and with beak that smote,
So shrieked through either throat
From the hot horror of its northern nest
That double-headed pest;
So, triple-crowned with fear and fraud and shame,
He of whom treason came,
The herdsman of the Gadarean swine;
So all his ravening kine,
Made fat with poisonous pasture; so not we,
Mother, beholding thee.
Make answer, O the crown of all our slain,
Ye that were one, being twain,
Twain brethren, twin-born to the second birth,
Chosen out of all our earth
To be the prophesying stars that say
How hard is night on day,

Stars in serene and sudden heaven rerisen
Before the sun break prison
And ere the moon be wasted; fair first flowers
In that red wreath of ours
Woven with the lives of all whose lives were shed
To crown their mother's head
With leaves of civic cypress and thick yew,
Till the olive bind it too,
Olive and laurel and all loftier leaves
That victory wears or weaves
At her fair feet for her beloved brow;
Hear, for she too hears now,
O Pisacane, from Calabrian sands;
O all heroic hands
Close on the sword-hilt, hands of all her dead;
O many a holy head,
Bowed for her sake even to her reddening dust;
O chosen, O pure and just,
Who counted for a small thing life's estate,
And died, and made it great;
Ye whose names mix with all her memories; ye
Who rather chose to see
Death, than our more intolerable things;
Thou whose name withers kings,
Agesilao; thou too, O chiefliest thou,
The slayer of splendid brow,
Laid where the lying lips of fear deride
The foiled tyrannicide,
Foiled, fallen, slain, scorned, and happy; being in fame,
Felice, like thy name,
Not like thy fortune; father of the fight,
Having in hand our light.
Ah, happy! for that sudden-swerving hand
Flung light on all thy land,
Yea, lit blind France with compulsory ray,
Driven down a righteous way;
Ah, happiest! for from thee the wars began,
From thee the fresh springs ran;
From thee the lady land that queens the earth
Gat as she gave new birth.
O sweet mute mouths, O all fair dead of ours,
Fair in her eyes as flowers,
Fair without feature, vocal without voice,
Strong without strength, rejoice!
Hear it with ears that hear not, and on eyes
That see not let it rise,
Rise as a sundawn; be it as dew that drips
On dumb and dusty lips;

Eyes have ye not, and see it; neither ears,
And there is none but hears.
This is the same for whom ye bled and wept;
She was not dead, but slept.
This is that very Italy which was
And is and shall not pass.

V

But thou, though all were not well done, O chief,
Must thou take shame or grief?
Because one man is not as thou or ten,
Must thou take shame for men?
Because the supreme sunrise is not yet,
Is the young dew not wet?
Wilt thou not yet abide a little while,
Soul without fear or guile,
Mazzini,—O our prophet, O our priest,
A little while at least?
A little hour of doubt and of control,
Sustain thy sacred soul;
Withhold thine heart, our father, but an hour;
Is it not here, the flower,
Is it not blown and fragrant from the root,
And shall not be the fruit?
Thy children, even thy people thou hast made,
Thine, with thy words arrayed,
Clothed with thy thoughts and girt with thy desires,
Yearn up toward thee as fires.
Art thou not father, O father, of all these?
From thine own Genoese
To where of nights the lower extreme lagune
Feels its Venetian moon,
Nor suckling's mouth nor mother's breast set free
But hath that grace through thee.
The milk of life on death's unnatural brink
Thou gavest them to drink,
The natural milk of freedom; and again
They drank, and they were men.
The wine and honey of freedom and of faith
They drank, and cast off death.
Bear with them now; thou art holier: yet endure,
Till they as thou be pure.
Their swords at least that stemmed half Austria's tide
Bade all its bulk divide;
Else, though fate bade them for a breath's space fall,
She had not fallen at all.

Not by their hands they made time's promise true;
Not by their hands, but through.
Nor on Custoza ran their blood to waste,
Nor fell their fame defaced
Whom stormiest Adria with tumultuous tides
Whirls undersea and hides.
Not his, who from the sudden-settling deck
Looked over death and wreck
To where the mother's bosom shone, who smiled
As he, so dying, her child;
For he smiled surely, dying, to mix his death
With her memorial breath;
Smiled, being most sure of her, that in no wise,
Die whoso will, she dies:
And she smiled surely, fair and far above,
Wept not, but smiled for love.
Thou too, O splendour of the sudden sword
That drove the crews abhorred
From Naples and the siren-footed strand,
Flash from thy master's hand,
Shine from the middle summer of the seas
To the old Aeolides,
Outshine their fiery fumes of burning night,
Sword, with thy midday light;
Flame as a beacon from the Tyrrhene foam
To the rent heart of Rome,
From the island of her lover and thy lord,
Her saviour and her sword.
In the fierce year of failure and of fame,
Art thou not yet the same
That wast as lightning swifter than all wings
In the blind face of kings?
When priests took counsel to devise despair,
And princes to forswear,
She clasped thee, O her sword and flag-bearer
And staff and shield to her,
O Garibaldi; need was hers and grief,
Of thee and of the chief,
And of another girt in arms to stand
As good of hope and hand,
As high of soul and happy, albeit indeed
The heart should burn and bleed,
So but the spirit shake not nor the breast
Swerve, but abide its rest.
As theirs did and as thine, though ruin clomb
The highest wall of Rome,
Though treason stained and spilt her lustral water,
And slaves led slaves to slaughter,

And priests, praying and slaying, watched them pass
From a strange France, alas,
That was not freedom; yet when these were past
Thy sword and thou stood fast,
Till new men seeing thee where Sicilian waves
Hear now no sound of slaves,
And where thy sacred blood is fragrant still
Upon the Bitter Hill,
Seeing by that blood one country saved and stained,
Less loved thee crowned than chained,
And less now only than the chief: for he,
Father of Italy,
Upbore in holy hands the babe new-born
Through loss and sorrow and scorn,
Of no man led, of many men reviled;
Till lo, the new-born child
Gone from between his hands, and in its place,
Lo, the fair mother's face.
Blessed is he of all men, being in one
As father to her and son,
Blessed of all men living, that he found
Her weak limbs bared and bound,
And in his arms and in his bosom bore,
And as a garment wore
Her weight of want, and as a royal dress
Put on her weariness.
As in faith's hoariest histories men read,
The strong man bore at need
Through roaring rapids when all heaven was wild
The likeness of a child
That still waxed greater and heavier as he trod,
And altered, and was God.
Praise him, O winds that move the molten air,
O light of days that were,
And light of days that shall be; land and sea,
And heaven and Italy:
Praise him, O storm and summer, shore and wave,
O skies and every grave;
O weeping hopes, O memories beyond tears,
O many and murmuring years,
O sounds far off in time and visions far,
O sorrow with thy star,
And joy with all thy beacons; ye that mourn,
And ye whose light is born;
O fallen faces, and O souls arisen,
Praise him from tomb and prison,
Praise him from heaven and sunlight; and ye floods,
And windy waves of woods;

Ye valleys and wild vineyards, ye lit lakes
And happier hillside brakes,
Untrampled by the accursed feet that trod
Fields golden from their god,
Fields of their god forsaken, whereof none
Sees his face in the sun,
Hears his voice from the floweriest wildernesses;
And, barren of his tresses,
Ye bays unplucked and laurels unentwined,
That no men break or bind,
And myrtles long forgetful of the sword,
And olives unadored,
Wisdom and love, white hands that save and slay,
Praise him; and ye as they,
Praise him, O gracious might of dews and rains
That feed the purple plains,
O sacred sunbeams bright as bare steel drawn,
O cloud and fire and dawn;
Red hills of flame, white Alps, green Apennines,
Banners of blowing pines,
Standards of stormy snows, flags of light leaves,
Three wherewith Freedom weaves
One ensign that once woven and once unfurled
Makes day of all a world,
Makes blind their eyes who knew not, and outbraves
The waste of iron waves;
Ye fields of yellow fullness, ye fresh fountains,
And mists of many mountains;
Ye moons and seasons, and ye days and nights;
Ye starry-headed heights,
And gorges melting sunward from the snow,
And all strong streams that flow,
Tender as tears, and fair as faith, and pure
As hearts made sad and sure
At once by many sufferings and one love;
O mystic deathless dove
Held to the heart of earth and in her hands
Cherished, O lily of lands,
White rose of time, dear dream of praises past—
For such as these thou wast,
That art as eagles setting to the sun,
As fawns that leap and run,
As a sword carven with keen floral gold,
Sword for an armed god's hold,
Flower for a crowned god's forehead—O our land,
Reach forth thine holiest hand,
O mother of many sons and memories,
Stretch out thine hand to his

That raised and gave thee life to run and leap
When thou wast full of sleep,
That touched and stung thee with young blood and breath
When thou wast hard on death.
Praise him, O all her cities and her crowns,
Her towers and thrones of towns;
O noblest Brescia, scarred from foot to head
And breast-deep in thy dead,
Praise him from all the glories of thy graves
That yellow Mela laves
With gentle and golden water, whose fair flood
Ran wider with thy blood:
Praise him, O born of that heroic breast,
O nursed thereat and blest,
Verona, fairer than thy mother fair,
But not more brave to bear:
Praise him, O Milan, whose imperial tread
Bruised once the German head;
Whose might, by northern swords left desolate,
Set foot on fear and fate:
Praise him, O long mute mouth of melodies,
Mantua, with louder keys,
With mightier chords of music even than rolled
From the large harps of old,
When thy sweet singer of golden throat and tongue,
Praising his tyrant, sung;
Though now thou sing not as of other days,
Learn late a better praise.
Not with the sick sweet lips of slaves that sing,
Praise thou no priest or king,
No brow-bound laurel of discoloured leaf,
But him, the crownless chief.
Praise him, O star of sun-forgotten times,
Among their creeds and crimes
That wast a fire of witness in the night,
Padua, the wise men's light:
Praise him, O sacred Venice, and the sea
That now exults through thee,
Full of the mighty morning and the sun,
Free of things dead and done;
Praise him from all the years of thy great grief,
That shook thee like a leaf
With winds and snows of torment, rain that fell
Red as the rains of hell,
Storms of black thunder and of yellow flame,
And all ill things but shame;
Praise him with all thy holy heart and strength;
Through thy walls' breadth and length

Praise him with all thy people, that their voice
Bid the strong soul rejoice,
The fair clear supreme spirit beyond stain,
Pure as the depth of pain,
High as the head of suffering, and secure
As all things that endure.
More than thy blind lord of an hundred years
Whose name our memory hears,
Home-bound from harbours of the Byzantine
Made tributary of thine,
Praise him who gave no gifts from oversea,
But gave thyself to thee.
O mother Genoa, through all years that run,
More than that other son,
Who first beyond the seals of sunset prest
Even to the unfooted west,
Whose back-blown flag scared from, their sheltering seas
The unknown Atlantides,
And as flame climbs through cloud and vapour clomb
Through streams of storm and foam,
Till half in sight they saw land heave and swim—
More than this man praise him.
One found a world new-born from virgin sea;
And one found Italy.
O heavenliest Florence, from the mouths of flowers
Fed by melodious hours,
From each sweet mouth that kisses light and air,
Thou whom thy fate made fair,
As a bound vine or any flowering tree,
Praise him who made thee free.
For no grape-gatherers trampling out the wine
Tread thee, the fairest vine;
For no man binds thee, no man bruises, none
Does with thee as these have done.
From where spring hears loud through her long lit vales
Triumphant nightingales,
In many a fold of fiery foliage hidden,
Withheld as things forbidden,
But clamorous with innumerable delight
In May's red, green, and white,
In the far-floated standard of the spring,
That bids men also sing,
Our flower of flags, our witness that we are free,
Our lamp for land and sea;
From where Majano feels through corn and vine
Spring move and melt as wine,
And Fiesole's embracing arms enclose
The immeasurable rose;

From hill-sides plumed with pine, and heights wind-worn
That feel the refluent morn,
Or where the moon's face warm and passionate
Burns, and men's hearts grow great,
And the swoln eyelids labour with sweet tears,
And in their burning ears
Sound throbs like flame, and in their eyes new light
Kindles the trembling night;
From faint illumined fields and starry valleys
Wherefrom the hill-wind sallies,
From Vallombrosa, from Valdarno raise
One Tuscan tune of praise.
O lordly city of the field of death,
Praise him with equal breath,
From sleeping streets and gardens, and the stream
That threads them as a dream
Threads without light the untravelled ways of sleep
With eyes that smile or weep;
From the sweet sombre beauty of wave and wall
That fades and does not fall;
From coloured domes and cloisters fair with fame,
Praise thou and thine his name.
Thou too, O little laurelled town of towers,
Clothed with the flame of flowers,
From windy ramparts girdled with young gold,
From thy sweet hillside fold
Of wallflowers and the acacia's belted bloom
And every blowing plume,
Halls that saw Dante speaking, chapels fair
As the outer hills and air,
Praise him who feeds the fire that Dante fed,
Our highest heroic head,
Whose eyes behold through floated cloud and flame
The maiden face of fame
Like April's in Valdelsa; fair as flowers,
And patient as the hours;
Sad with slow sense of time, and bright with faith
That levels life and death;
The final fame, that with a foot sublime
Treads down reluctant time;
The fame that waits and watches and is wise,
A virgin with chaste eyes,
A goddess who takes hands with great men's grief;
Praise her, and him, our chief.
Praise him, O Siena, and thou her deep green spring,
O Fonte Branda, sing:
Shout from the red clefts of thy fiery crags,
Shake out thy flying flags

In the long wind that streams from hill to hill;
Bid thy full music fill
The desolate red waste of sunset air
And fields the old time saw fair,
But now the hours ring void through ruined lands,
Wild work of mortal hands;
Yet through thy dead Maremma let his name
Take flight and pass in flame,
And the red ruin of disastrous hours
Shall quicken into flowers.
Praise him, O fiery child of sun and sea,
Naples, who bade thee be;
For till he sent the swords that scourge and save,
Thou wast not, but thy grave.
But more than all these praise him and give thanks,
Thou, from thy Tiber's banks,
From all thine hills and from thy supreme dome,
Praise him, O risen Rome.
Let all thy children cities at thy knee
Lift up their voice with thee,
Saying 'for thy love's sake and our perished grief
We laud thee, O our chief;'
Saying 'for thine hand and help when hope was dead
We thank thee, O our head;'
Saying 'for thy voice and face within our sight
We bless thee, O our light;
For waters cleansing us from days defiled
We praise thee, O our child.'

VI

So with an hundred cities' mouths in one
Praising thy supreme son,
Son of thy sorrow, O mother, O maid and mother,
Our queen, who serve none other,
Our lady of pity and mercy, and full of grace,
Turn otherwhere thy face,
Turn for a little and look what things are these
Now fallen before thy knees;
Turn upon them thine eyes who hated thee,
Behold what things they be,
Italia: these are stubble that were steel,
Dust, or a turning wheel;
As leaves, as snow, as sand, that were so strong;
And howl, for all their song,
And wail, for all their wisdom; they that were
So great, they are all stript bare,

They are all made empty of beauty, and all abhorred;
They are shivered and their sword;
They are slain who slew, they are heartless who were wise;
Yea, turn on these thine eyes,
O thou, soliciting with soul sublime
The obscure soul of time,
Thou, with the wounds thy holy body bears
From broken swords of theirs,
Thou, with the sweet swoln eyelids that have bled
Tears for thy thousands dead,
And upon these, whose swords drank up like dew
The sons of thine they slew,
These, whose each gun blasted with murdering mouth
Live flowers of thy fair south,
These, whose least evil told in alien ears
Turned men's whole blood to tears,
These, whose least sin remembered for pure shame
Turned all those tears to flame,
Even upon these, when breaks the extreme blow
And all the world cries woe,
When heaven reluctant rains long-suffering fire
On these and their desire,
When his wind shakes them and his waters whelm
Who rent thy robe and realm,
When they that poured thy dear blood forth as wine
Pour forth their own for thine,
On these, on these have mercy: not in hate,
But full of sacred fate,
Strong from the shrine and splendid from the god,
Smite, with no second rod.
Because they spared not, do thou rather spare:
Be not one thing they were.
Let not one tongue of theirs who hate thee say
That thou wast even as they.
Because their hands were bloody, be thine white;
Show light where they shed night:
Because they are foul, be thou the rather pure;
Because they are feeble, endure;
Because they had no pity, have thou pity.
And thou, O supreme city,
O priestless Rome that shall be, take in trust
Their names, their deeds, their dust,
Who held life less than thou wert; be the least
To thee indeed a priest,
Priest and burnt-offering and blood-sacrifice
Given without prayer or price,
A holier immolation than men wist,
A costlier eucharist,

A sacrament more saving; bend thine head
Above these many dead
Once, and salute with thine eternal eyes
Their lowest head that lies.
Speak from thy lips of immemorial speech
If but one word for each.
Kiss but one kiss on each thy dead son's mouth
Fallen dumb or north or south.
And laying but once thine hand on brow and breast,
Bless them, through whom thou art blest.
And saying in ears of these thy dead, "Well done,"
Shall they not hear "O son"?
And bowing thy face to theirs made pale for thee,
Shall the shut eyes not see?
Yea, through the hollow-hearted world of death,
As light, as blood, as breath,
Shall there not flash and flow the fiery sense,
The pulse of prescience?
Shall not these know as in times overpast
Thee loftiest to the last?
For times and wars shall change, kingdoms and creeds,
And dreams of men, and deeds;
Earth shall grow grey with all her golden things,
Pale peoples and hoar kings;
But though her thrones and towers of nations fall,
Death has no part in all;
In the air, nor in the imperishable sea,
Nor heaven, nor truth, nor thee.
Yea, let all sceptre-stricken nations lie,
But live thou though they die;
Let their flags fade as flowers that storm can mar,
But thine be like a star;
Let England's, if it float not for men free,
Fall, and forget the sea;
Let France's, if it shadow a hateful head,
Drop as a leaf drops dead;
Thine let what storm soever smite the rest
Smite as it seems him best;
Thine let the wind that can, by sea or land,
Wrest from thy banner-hand.
Die they in whom dies freedom, die and cease,
Though the world weep for these;
Live thou and love and lift when these lie dead
The green and white and red.

VII

O our Republic that shalt bind in bands
The kingdomless far lands
And link the chainless ages; thou that wast
With England ere she past
Among the faded nations, and shalt be
Again, when sea to sea
Calls through the wind and light of morning time,
And throneless clime to clime
Makes antiphonal answer; thou that art
Where one man's perfect heart
Burns, one man's brow is brightened for thy sake,
Thine, strong to make or break;
O fair Republic hallowing with stretched hands
The limitless free lands,
When all men's heads for love, not fear, bow down
To thy sole royal crown,
As thou to freedom; when man's life smells sweet,
And at thy bright swift feet
A bloodless and a bondless world is laid;
Then, when thy men are made,
Let these indeed as we in dreams behold
One chosen of all thy fold,
One of all fair things fairest, one exalt
Above all fear or fault,
One unforgetful of unhappier men
And us who loved her then;
With eyes that outlook suns and dream on graves;
With voice like quiring waves;
With heart the holier for their memories' sake
Who slept that she might wake;
With breast the sweeter for that sweet blood lost,
And all the milkless cost;
Lady of earth, whose large equality
Bends but to her and thee;
Equal with heaven, and infinite of years,
And splendid from quenched tears;
Strong with old strength of great things fallen and fled,
Diviner for her dead;
Chaste of all stains and perfect from all scars,
Above all storms and stars,
All winds that blow through time, all waves that foam,
Our Capitolian Rome.

1867.

ODE ON THE PROCLAMATION OF THE FRENCH REPUBLIC

To: VICTOR HUGO

STROPHE 1

With songs and crying and sounds of acclamations,
Lo, the flame risen, the fire that falls in showers!
Hark; for the word is out among the nations:
Look; for the light is up upon the hours:
O fears, O shames, O many tribulations,
Yours were all yesterdays, but this day ours.
Strong were your bonds linked fast with lamentations,
With groans and tears built into walls and towers;
Strong were your works and wonders of high stations,
Your forts blood-based, and rampires of your powers:
Lo now the last of divers desolations,
The hand of time, that gathers hosts like flowers;
Time, that fills up and pours out generations;
Time, at whose breath confounded empire cowers.

STROPHE 2

What are these moving in the dawn's red gloom?
What is she waited on by dread and doom,
Ill ministers of morning, bondmen born of night?
If that head veiled and bowed be morning's head,
If she come walking between doom and dread,
Who shall rise up with song and dance before her sight?

Are not the night's dead heaped about her feet?
Is not death swollen, and slaughter full of meat?
What, is their feast a bride-feast, where men sing and dance?
A bitter, a bitter bride-song and a shrill
Should the house raise that such bride-followers fill,
Wherein defeat weds ruin, and takes for bride-bed France.

For nineteen years deep shame and sore desire
Fed from men's hearts with hungering fangs of fire,
And hope fell sick with famine for the food of change.
Now is change come, but bringing funeral urns;
Now is day nigh, but the dawn blinds and burns;
Now time long dumb hath language, but the tongue is strange.

We that have seen her not our whole lives long,
We to whose ears her dirge was cradle-song,
The dirge men sang who laid in earth her living head,
Is it by such light that we live to see

Rise, with rent hair and raiment, Liberty?
Does her grave open only to restore her dead?

Ah, was it this we looked for, looked and prayed,
This hour that treads upon the prayers we made,
This ravening hour that breaks down good and ill alike?
Ah, was it thus we thought to see her and hear,
The one love indivisible and dear?
Is it her head that hands which strike down wrong must strike?

STROPHE 3

Where is hope, and promise where, in all these things,
Shocks of strength with strength, and jar of hurtling kings?
Who of all men, who will show us any good?
Shall these lightnings of blind battles give men light?
Where is freedom? who will bring us in her sight,
That have hardly seen her footprint where she stood?

STROPHE 4

Who is this that rises red with wounds and splendid,
All her breast and brow made beautiful with scars,
Burning bare as naked daylight, undefended,
In her hands for spoils her splintered prison-bars,
In her eyes the light and fire of long pain ended,
In her lips a song as of the morning stars?

STROPHE 5

O torn out of thy trance,
O deathless, O my France,
O many-wounded mother, O redeemed to reign!
O rarely sweet and bitter
The bright brief tears that glitter
On thine unclosing eyelids, proud of their own pain;
The beautiful brief tears
That wash the stains of years
White as the names immortal of thy chosen and slain.
O loved so much so long,
O smitten with such wrong,
O purged at last and perfect without spot or stain,
Light of the light of man,
Reborn republican,
At last, O first Republic, hailed in heaven again!

Out of the obscene eclipse
Rerisen, with burning lips
To witness for us if we looked for thee in vain.

Thou wast the light whereby men saw
Light, thou the trumpet of the law
Proclaiming manhood to mankind;
And what if all these years were blind
And shameful? Hath the sun a flaw
Because one hour hath power to draw
Mist round him wreathed as links to bind?
And what if now keen anguish drains
The very wellspring of thy veins
And very spirit of thy breath?
The life outlives them and disdains;
The sense which makes the soul remains,
And blood of thought which travaileth
To bring forth hope with procreant pains.
O thou that satest bound in chains
Between thine hills and pleasant plains
As whom his own soul vanquisheth,
Held in the bonds of his own thought,
Whence very death can take off nought,
Nor sleep, with bitterer dreams than death,
What though thy thousands at thy knees
Lie thick as grave-worms feed on these,
Though thy green fields and joyous places
Are populous with blood-blackening faces
And wan limbs eaten by the sun?
Better an end of all men's races,
Better the world's whole work were done,
And life wiped out of all our traces,
And there were left to time not one,
Than such as these that fill thy graves
Should sow in slaves the seed of slaves.

Not of thy sons, O mother many-wounded,
Not of thy sons are slaves ingrafted and grown.
Was it not thine, the fire whence light rebounded
From kingdom on rekindling kingdom thrown,
From hearts confirmed on tyrannies confounded,
From earth on heaven, fire mightier than his own?

Not thine the breath wherewith time's clarion sounded,
And all the terror in the trumpet blown?
The voice whereat the thunders stood astounded
As at a new sound of a God unknown?
And all the seas and shores within them bounded
Shook at the strange speech of thy lips alone,
And all the hills of heaven, the storm-surrounded,
Trembled, and all the night sent forth a groan.

ANTISTROPHE 2

What hast thou done that such an hour should be
More than another clothed with blood to thee?
Thou hast seen many a bloodred hour before this one.
What art thou that thy lovers should misdoubt?
What is this hour that it should cast hope out?
If hope turn back and fall from thee, what hast thou done?

Thou hast done ill against thine own soul; yea,
Thine own soul hast thou slain and burnt away,
Dissolving it with poison into foul thin fume.
Thine own life and creation of thy fate
Thou hast set thine hand to unmake and discreate;
And now thy slain soul rises between dread and doom.

Yea, this is she that comes between them led;
That veiled head is thine own soul's buried head,
The head that was as morning's in the whole world's sight.
These wounds are deadly on thee, but deadlier
Those wounds the ravenous poison left on her;
How shall her weak hands hold thy weak hands up to fight?

Ah, but her fiery eyes, her eyes are these
That, gazing, make thee shiver to the knees
And the blood leap within thee, and the strong joy rise.
What, doth her sight yet make thine heart to dance?
O France, O freedom, O the soul of France,
Are ye then quickened, gazing in each other's eyes?

Ah, and her words, the words wherewith she sought thee
Sorrowing, and bare in hand the robe she wrought thee
To wear when soul and body were again made one,
And fairest among women, and a bride,
Sweet-voiced to sing the bridegroom to her side,
The spirit of man, the bridegroom brighter than the sun!

ANTISTROPHE 3

Who shall help me? who shall take me by the hand?
Who shall teach mine eyes to see, my feet to stand,
Now my foes have stripped and wounded me by night?
Who shall heal me? who shall come to take my part?
Who shall set me as a seal upon his heart,
As a seal upon his arm made bare for fight?

ANTISTROPHE 4

If thou know not, O thou fairest among women,
If thou see not where the signs of him abide,
Lift thine eyes up to the light that stars grow dim in,
To the morning whence he comes to take thy side.
None but he can bear the light that love wraps him in,
When he comes on earth to take himself a bride.

ANTISTROPHE 5

Light of light, name of names,
Whose shadows are live flames,
The soul that moves the wings of worlds upon their way;
Life, spirit, blood and breath
In time and change and death
Substant through strength and weakness, ardour and decay;
Lord of the lives of lands,
Spirit of man, whose hands
Weave the web through wherein man's centuries fall as prey;
That art within our will
Power to make, save, and kill,
Knowledge and choice, to take extremities and weigh;
In the soul's hand to smite
Strength, in the soul's eye sight;
That to the soul art even as is the soul to clay;
Now to this people be
Love; come, to set them free,
With feet that tread the night, with eyes that sound the day.

ANTISTROPHE 6

Thou that wast on their fathers dead
As effluent God effused and shed,
Heaven to be handled, hope made flesh,
Break for them now time's iron mesh;

Give them thyself for hand and head,
Thy breath for life, thy love for bread,
Thy thought for spirit to refresh,
Thy bitterness to pierce and sting,
Thy sweetness for a healing spring.
Be to them knowledge, strength, life, light,
Thou to whose feet the centuries cling
And in the wide warmth of thy wing
Seek room and rest as birds by night,
O thou the kingless people's king,
To whom the lips of silence sing,
Called by thy name of thanksgiving
Freedom, and by thy name of might
Justice, and by thy secret name
Love; the same need is on the same
Men, be the same God in their sight!
From this their hour of bloody tears
Their praise goes up into thine ears,
Their bruised lips clothe thy name with praises,
The song of thee their crushed voice raises,
Their grief seeks joy for psalms to borrow,
With tired feet seeks her through time's mazes
Where each day's blood leaves pale the morrow,
And from their eyes in thine there gazes
A spirit other far than sorrow—
A soul triumphal, white and whole
And single, that salutes thy soul.

EPODE

All the lights of the sweet heaven that sing together;
All the years of the green earth that bare man free;
Rays and lightnings of the fierce or tender weather,
Heights and lowlands, wastes and headlands of the sea,
Dawns and sunsets, hours that hold the world in tether,
Be our witnesses and seals of things to be.
Lo the mother, the Republic universal,
Hands that hold time fast, hands feeding men with might,
Lips that sing the song of the earth, that make rehearsal
Of all seasons, and the sway of day with night,
Eyes that see as from a mountain the dispersal,
The huge ruin of things evil, and the flight;
Large exulting limbs, and bosom godlike moulded
Where the man-child hangs, and womb wherein he lay;
Very life that could it die would leave the soul dead,
Face whereat all fears and forces flee away,
Breath that moves the world as winds a flower-bell folded,

Feet that trampling the gross darkness beat out day.
In the hour of pain and pity,
Sore spent, a wounded city,
Her foster-child seeks to her, stately where she stands;
In the utter hour of woes,
Wind-shaken, blind with blows,
Paris lays hold upon her, grasps her with child's hands;
Face kindles face with fire,
Hearts take and give desire,
Strange joy breaks red as tempest on tormented lands.
Day to day, man to man,
Plights love republican,
And faith and memory burn with passion toward each other;
Hope, with fresh heavens to track,
Looks for a breath's space back,
Where the divine past years reach hands to this their brother;
And souls of men whose death
Was light to her and breath
Send word of love yet living to the living mother.
They call her, and she hears;
O France, thy marvellous years,
The years of the strong travail, the triumphant time,
Days terrible with love,
Red-shod with flames thereof,
Call to this hour that breaks in pieces crown and crime;
The hour with feet to spurn,
Hands to crush, fires to burn
The state whereto no latter foot of man shall climb.
Yea, come what grief, now may
By ruinous night or day,
One grief there cannot, one the first and last grief, shame.
Come force to break thee and bow
Down, shame can come not now,
Nor, though hands wound thee, tongues make mockery of thy name:
Come swords and scar thy brow,
No brand there burns it now,
No spot but of thy blood marks thy white-fronted fame.
Now, though the mad blind morrow
With shafts of iron sorrow
Should split thine heart, and whelm thine head with sanguine waves;
Though all that draw thy breath
Bled from all veins to death,
And thy dead body were the grave of all their graves,
And thine unchilded womb
For all their tombs a tomb,
At least within thee as on thee room were none for slaves.
This power thou hast, to be,
Come death or come not, free;

That in all tongues of time's this praise be chanted of thee,
That in thy wild worst hour
This power put in thee power,
And moved as hope around and hung as heaven above thee,
And while earth sat in sadness
In only thee put gladness,
Put strength and love, to make all hearts of ages love thee.
That in death's face thy chant
Arose up jubilant,
And thy great heart with thy great peril grew more great:
And sweet for bitter tears
Put out the fires of fears,
And love made lovely for thee loveless hell and hate;
And they that house with error,
Cold shame and burning terror,
Fled from truth risen and thee made mightier than thy fate.
This shall all years remember;
For this thing shall September
Have only name of honour, only sign of white.
And this year's fearful name,
France, in thine house of fame
Above all names of all thy triumphs shalt thou write,
When, seeing thy freedom stand
Even at despair's right hand,
The cry thou gavest at heart was only of delight.

DIRAE

Guai a voi, anime prave.
Dante.

Soyez maudits, d'abord d'être ce que vous êtes,
Et puis soyez maudits d'obséder les poëtes!
Victor Hugo.

I

A DEAD KING

Ferdinand II entered Malebolge May 22nd, 1859.

Go down to hell. This end is good to see;
The breath is lightened and the sense at ease
Because thou art not; sense nor breath there is

In what thy body was, whose soul shall be
Chief nerve of hell's pained heart eternally.
Thou art abolished from the midst of these
That are what thou wast: Pius from his knees
Blows off the dust that flecked them, bowed for thee.
Yea, now the long-tongued slack-lipped litanies
Fail, and the priest has no more prayer to sell—
Now the last Jesuit found about thee is
The beast that made thy fouler flesh his cell—
Time lays his finger on thee, saying, "Cease;
Here is no room for thee; go down to hell."

II

A YEAR AFTER

If blood throbs yet in this that was thy face,
O thou whose soul was full of devil's faith,
If in thy flesh the worm's bite slackeneth
In some acute red pause of iron days,
Arise now, gird thee, get thee on thy ways,
Breathe off the worm that crawls and fears not breath;
King, it may be thou shalt prevail on death;
King, it may be thy soul shall find out grace.
O spirit that hast eased the place of Cain,
Weep now and howl, yea weep now sore; for this
That was thy kingdom hath spat out its king.
Wilt thou plead now with God? behold again,
Thy prayer for thy son's sake is turned to a hiss,
Thy mouth to a snake's whose slime outlives the sting,

III

PETER'S PENCE FROM PERUGIA

Iscariot, thou grey-grown beast of blood,
Stand forth to plead; stand, while red drops run here
And there down fingers shaken with foul fear,
Down the sick shivering chin that stooped and sued,
Bowed to the bosom, for a little food
At Herod's hand, who smites thee cheek and ear.
Cry out, Iscariot; haply he will hear;
Cry, till he turn again to do thee good.
Gather thy gold up, Judas, all thy gold,
And buy thee death; no Christ is here to sell,
But the dead earth of poor men bought and sold,

While year heaps year above thee safe in hell,
To grime thy grey dishonourable head
With dusty shame, when thou art damned and dead.

IV

PAPAL ALLOCUTION

"Popule mi, quid tibi feci?"

What hast thou done? Hark, till thine ears wax hot,
Judas; for these and these things hast thou done.
Thou hast made earth faint, and sickened the sweet sun,
With fume of blood that reeks from limbs that rot;
Thou hast washed thine hands and mouth, saying, "Am I not
Clean?" and thy lips were bloody, and there was none
To speak for man against thee, no, not one;
This hast thou done to us, Iscariot.
Therefore, though thou be deaf and heaven be dumb,
A cry shall be from under to proclaim
In the ears of all who shed men's blood or sell
Pius the Ninth, Judas the Second, come
Where Boniface out of the filth and flame
Barks for his advent in the clefts of hell. (i)

(i) Dante, "Inferno," xix. 53.

V

THE BURDEN OF AUSTRIA

1866

O daughter of pride, wasted with misery,
With all the glory that thy shame put on
Stripped off thy shame, O daughter of Babylon,
Yea, whoso be it, yea, happy shall he be
That as thou hast served us hath rewarded thee.
Blessed, who throweth against war's boundary stone
Thy warrior brood, and breaketh bone by bone
Misrule thy son, thy daughter Tyranny.
That landmark shalt thou not remove for shame,
But sitting down there in a widow's weed
Wail; for what fruit is now of thy red fame?
Have thy sons too and daughters learnt indeed
What thing it is to weep, what thing to bleed?

Is it not thou that now art but a name? (ii)

(ii) "A geographical expression."—Metternich of Italy.

VI

LOCUSTA

Come close and see her and hearken. This is she.
Stop the ways fast against the stench that nips
Your nostril as it nears her. Lo, the lips
That between prayer and prayer find time to be
Poisonous, the hands holding a cup and key,
Key of deep hell, cup whence blood reeks and drips;
The loose lewd limbs, the reeling hingeless hips,
The scurf that is not skin but leprosy.
This haggard harlot grey of face and green
With the old hand's cunning mixes her new priest
The cup she mixed her Nero, stirred and spiced.
She lisps of Mary and Jesus Nazarene
With a tongue tuned, and head that bends to the east,
Praying. There are who say she is bride of Christ.

VII

CELAENO

The blind king hides his weeping eyeless head,
Sick with the helpless hate and shame and awe,
Till food have choked the glutted hell-bird's craw
And the foul cropful creature lie as dead
And soil itself with sleep and too much bread:
So the man's life serves under the beast's law,
And things whose spirit lives in mouth and maw
Share shrieking the soul's board and soil her bed,
Till man's blind spirit, their sick slave, resign
Its kingdom to the priests whose souls are swine,
And the scourged serf lie reddening from their rod,
Discrowned, disrobed, dismantled, with lost eyes
Seeking where lurks in what conjectural skies
That triple-headed hound of hell their God.

VIII

A CHOICE

Faith is the spirit that makes man's body and blood
Sacred, to crown when life and death have ceased
His heavenward head for high fame's holy feast;
But as one swordstroke swift as wizard's rod
Made Caesar carrion and made Brutus God,
Faith false or true, born patriot or born priest,
Smites into semblance or of man or beast
The soul that feeds on clean or unclean food.
Lo here the faith that lives on its own light,
Visible music; and lo there, the foul
Shape without shape, the harpy throat and howl.
Sword of the spirit of man! arise and smite,
And sheer through throat and claw and maw and tongue
Kill the beast faith that lives on its own dung.

IX

THE AUGURS

Lay the corpse out on the altar; bid the elect
Slaves clear the ways of service spiritual,
Sweep clean the stalled soul's serviceable stall,
Ere the chief priest's dismantling hands detect
The ulcerous flesh of faith all scaled and specked
Beneath the bandages that hid it all,
And with sharp edgetools oecumenical
The leprous carcases of creeds dissect.
As on the night ere Brutus grew divine
The sick-souled augurs found their ox or swine
Heartless; so now too by their after art
In the same Rome, at an uncleaner shrine,
Limb from rank limb, and putrid part from part,
They carve the corpse—a beast without a heart.

X

A COUNSEL

O strong Republic of the nobler years
Whose white feet shine beside time's fairer flood
That shall flow on the clearer for our blood
Now shed, and the less brackish for our tears;
When time and truth have put out hopes and fears
With certitude, and love has burst the bud,
If these whose powers then down the wind shall scud

Still live to feel thee smite their eyes and ears,
When thy foot's tread hath crushed their crowns and creeds,
Care thou not then to crush the beast that bleeds,
The snake whose belly cleaveth to the sod,
Nor set thine heel on men as on their deeds;
But let the worm Napoleon crawl untrod,
Nor grant Mastai the gallows of his God.

1869.

XI

THE MODERATES

Virtutem videant intabescantque relicta.

She stood before her traitors bound and bare,
Clothed with her wounds and with her naked shame
As with a weed of fiery tears and flame,
Their mother-land, their common weal and care,
And they turned from her and denied, and sware
They did not know this woman nor her name.
And they took truce with tyrants and grew tame,
And gathered up cast crowns and creeds to wear,
And rags and shards regilded. Then she took
In her bruised hands their broken pledge, and eyed
These men so late so loud upon her side
With one inevitable and tearless look,
That they might see her face whom they forsook;
And they beheld what they had left, and died.

February 1870.

XII

INTERCESSION

Ave Caesar Imperator, moriturum te saluto.

I

O Death, a little more, and then the worm;
A little longer, O Death, a little yet,
Before the grave gape and the grave-worm fret;
Before the sanguine-spotted hand infirm
Be rottenness, and that foul brain, the germ

Of all ill things and thoughts, be stopped and set;
A little while, O Death, ere he forget,
A small space more of life, a little term;
A little longer ere he and thou be met,
Ere in that hand that fed thee to thy mind
The poison-cup of life be overset;
A little respite of disastrous breath,
Till the soul lift up her lost eyes, and find
Nor God nor help nor hope, but thee, O Death.

II

Shall a man die before his dying day,
Death? and for him though the utter day be nigh,
Not yet, not yet we give him leave to die;
We give him grace not yet that men should say
He is dead, wiped out, perished and past away.
Till the last bitterness of life go by,
Thou shalt not slay him; till those last dregs run dry,
O thou last lord of life! thou shalt not slay.
Let the lips live a little while and lie,
The hand a little, and falter, and fail of strength,
And the soul shudder and sicken at the sky;
Yea, let him live, though God nor man would let
Save for the curse' sake; then at bitter length,
Lord, will we yield him to thee, but not yet.

III

Hath he not deeds to do and days to see
Yet ere the day that is to see him dead?
Beats there no brain yet in the poisonous head,
Throbs there no treason? if no such thing there be,
If no such thought, surely this is not he.
Look to the hands then; are the hands not red?
What are the shadows about this man's bed?
Death, was not this the cupbearer to thee?
Nay, let him live then, till in this life's stead
Even he shall pray for that thou hast to give;
Till seeing his hopes and not his memories fled
Even he shall cry upon thee a bitter cry,
That life is worse than death; then let him live,
Till death seem worse than life; then let him die.

IV

O watcher at the guardless gate of kings,
O doorkeeper that serving at their feast
Hast in thine hand their doomsday drink, and seest
With eyeless sight the soul of unseen things;
Thou in whose ear the dumb time coming sings,
Death, priest and king that makest of king and priest
A name, a dream, a less thing than the least,
Hover awhile above him with closed wings,
Till the coiled soul, an evil snake-shaped beast,
Eat its base bodily lair of flesh away;
If haply, or ever its cursed life have ceased,
Or ever thy cold hands cover his head
From sight of France and freedom and broad day,
He may see these and wither and be dead.

Paris: September 1869.

XIII

THE SAVIOUR OF SOCIETY

I

O son of man, but of what man who knows?
That broughtest healing on thy leathern wings
To priests, and under them didst gather kings,
And madest friends to thee of all man's foes;
Before thine incarnation, the tale goes,
Thy virgin mother, pure of sensual stings,
Communed by night with angels of chaste things,
And, full of grace, untimely felt the throes
Of motherhood upon her, and believed
The obscure annunciation made when late
A raven-feathered raven-throated dove
Croaked salutation to the mother of love
Whose misconception was immaculate,
And when her time was come she misconceived.

II

Thine incarnation was upon this wise,
Saviour; and out of east and west were led
To thy foul cradle by thy planet red
Shepherds of souls that feed their sheep with lies
Till the utter soul die as the body dies,

And the wise men that ask but to be fed
Though the hot shambles be their board and bed
And sleep on any dunghill shut their eyes,
So they lie warm and fatten in the mire:
And the high priest enthroned yet in thy name,
Judas, baptised thee with men's blood for hire;
And now thou hangest nailed to thine own shame
In sight of all time, but while heaven has flame
Shalt find no resurrection from hell-fire.

December 1869.

XIV

MENTANA: SECOND ANNIVERSARY

Est-ce qu'il n'est pas temps que la foudre se prouve,
Cieux profonds, en broyant ce chien, fils de la louve?
La Légende des Siècles:—Ratbert.

I

By the dead body of Hope, the spotless lamb
Thou threwest into the high priest's slaughtering-room,
And by the child Despair born red therefrom
As, thank the secret sire picked out to cram
With spurious spawn thy misconceiving dam,
Thou, like a worm from a town's common tomb,
Didst creep from forth the kennel of her womb,
Born to break down with catapult and ram
Man's builded towers of promise, and with breath
And tongue to track and hunt his hopes to death:
O, by that sweet dead body abused and slain,
And by that child mismothered,—dog, by all
Thy curses thou hast cursed mankind withal,
With what curse shall man curse thee back again?

II

By the brute soul that made man's soul its food;
By time grown poisonous with it; by the hate
And horror of all souls not miscreate;
By the hour of power that evil hath on good;
And by the incognizable fatherhood
Which made a whorish womb the shameful gate

That opening let out loose to fawn on fate
A hound half-blooded ravening for man's blood;
(What prayer but this for thee should any say,
Thou dog of hell, but this that Shakespeare said?)
By night deflowered and desecrated day,
That fall as one curse on one cursed head,
"Cancel his bond of life, dear God, I pray,
That I may live to say, The dog is dead!"

1869.

XV

MENTANA: THIRD ANNIVERSARY

I

Such prayers last year were put up for thy sake;
What shall this year do that hath lived to see
The piteous and unpitied end of thee?
What moan, what cry, what clamour shall it make,
Seeing as a reed breaks all thine empire break,
And all thy great strength as a rotten tree,
Whose branches made broad night from sea to sea,
And the world shuddered when a leaf would shake?
From the unknown deep wherein those prayers were heard,
From the dark height of time there sounds a word,
Crying, Comfort; though death ride on this red hour,
Hope waits with eyes that make the morning dim,
Till liberty, reclothed with love and power,
Shall pass and know not if she tread on him.

II

The hour for which men hungered and had thirst,
And dying were loth to die before it came,
Is it indeed upon thee? and the lame
Late foot of vengeance on thy trace accurst
For years insepulchred and crimes inhearsed,
For days marked red or black with blood or shame,
Hath it outrun thee to tread out thy name?
This scourge, this hour, is this indeed the worst?
O clothed and crowned with curses, canst thou tell?
Have thy dead whispered to thee what they see
Whose eyes are open in the dark on thee

Ere spotted soul and body take farewell
Or what of life beyond the worm's may be
Satiate the immitigable hours in hell?

1870.

XVI

THE DESCENT INTO HELL

January 9th, 1873

I

O Night and death, to whom we grudged him then,
When in man's sight he stood not yet undone,
Your king, your priest, your saviour, and your son,
We grudge not now, who know that not again
Shall this curse come upon the sins of men,
Nor this face look upon the living sun
That shall behold not so abhorred an one
In all the days whereof his eye takes ken.
The bond is cancelled, and the prayer is heard
That seemed so long but weak and wasted breath;
Take him, for he is yours, O night and death.
Hell yawns on him whose life was as a word
Uttered by death in hate of heaven and light,
A curse now dumb upon the lips of night.

II

What shapes are these and shadows without end
That fill the night full as a storm of rain
With myriads of dead men and women slain,
Old with young, child with mother, friend with friend,
That on the deep mid wintering air impend,
Pale yet with mortal wrath and human pain,
Who died that this man dead now too might reign,
Toward whom their hands point and their faces bend?
The ruining flood would redden earth and air
If for each soul whose guiltless blood was shed
There fell but one drop on this one man's head
Whose soul to-night stands bodiless and bare,
For whom our hearts give thanks who put up prayer,
That we have lived to say, The dog is dead.

APOLOGIA

If wrath embitter the sweet mouth of song,
And make the sunlight fire before those eyes
That would drink draughts of peace from the unsoiled skies,
The wrongdoing is not ours, but ours the wrong,
Who hear too loud on earth and see too long
The grief that dies not with the groan that dies,
Till the strong bitterness of pity cries
Within us, that our anger should be strong.
For chill is known by heat and heat by chill,
And the desire that hope makes love to still
By the fear flying beside it or above,
A falcon fledged to follow a fledgeling dove,
And by the fume and flame of hate of ill
The exuberant light and burning bloom of love.

Algernon Charles Swinburne – A Short Biography

Algernon Charles Swinburne was born at 7 Chester Street, Grosvenor Place, in London, on April 5th,
1837. He was the eldest of six children born to Captain Charles Henry Swinburne and Lady Jane
Henrietta, daughter of the 3rd Earl of Ashburnham, a wealthy Northumbrian family.

Swinburne spent his early years at East Dene in Bonchurch, on the Isle of Wight. As a child, Swinburne
was nervous and frail, but also imbued with a nervous energy and fearlessness almost to the point of
recklessness.

He was schooled at Eton College from 1849 to 1853. It was here that he first began to write poetry. He
excelled at languages and whilst still at Eton won first prizes in both French and Italian.

From Eton he moved to Oxford where he attended at Balliol College from 1856. Here he met friends to
whom he became closely attached, among them Dante Gabriel Rossetti, William Morris and Edward
Burne-Jones, who in 1857, were painting their Arthurian murals on the walls of the Oxford Union. At
Oxford Swinburne was mentored by Benjamin Jowett, the master of Balliol College, who recognised his
poetic talent and, intervening on his behalf, tried to keep him from being expelled when he celebrated
the Italian patriot Orsini, and his failed attempt on the life of Napoleon III in 1858. Swinburne had to
leave the Universcity for a few months due to this but returned in May, 1860 but never received a
degree.

Summers were usually spent at Capheaton Hall in Northumberland, the house of his grandfather, Sir John Swinburne, 6th Baronet, who had a famous library and was himself President of the Literary and Philosophical Society in Newcastle upon Tyne.

Swinburne proudly considered himself a native of Northumberland and this is reflected in poems such as the intensely patriotic 'Northumberland' and 'Grace Darling'. He enjoyed riding across the moors and was, it was said, a daring horseman, as he moved 'through honeyed leagues of the northland border', as he remembered the Scottish border in his Recollections.

In the period from 1857 to 1860, Swinburne was one of a number of Pre-Raphaelite's who visited and became part of Lady Pauline Trevelyan's intellectual circle at Wallington Hall, a few miles west of Morpeth in Northumberland.

After leaving college, he moved to London and began his career in earnest as well as becoming a constant visitor to the Rossetti's house. To Rossetti Swinburne was his 'little Northumbrian friend', an affectionate reference to Swinburne's small stature—a mere five foot four. Whatever Swinburne lacked in height he made up for in poetic talent. However, with the burden of such great talent came the unveiling of a dark side that was to cause him pain and would, at times, threaten his very existence with all manner of self-inflicted pains through drink, drugs and sado-machoism.

In 1860 Swinburne published two verse dramas; The Queen Mother and Rosamond but it would not be until 1865 that Swinburne would achieve literary success with Atalanta in Calydon.

In 1861, Swinburne visited Menton on the French Riviera to recover from the effects of yet another period of excess use of alcohol, staying at the Villa Laurenti. From Menton, Swinburne then travelled on to Italy, where he journeyed widely.

After Elizabeth Rossetti's death from suicide in 1862, he and Rossetti moved to Tudor House at 16 Cheyne Walk in Chelsea. The stories that survive from his year with Rossetti are typical Swinburne. In one, Rossetti once had to tell him to keep down the noise — he and a boyfriend had been sliding naked down the bannisters and disturbing Rossetti's painting. He took a sardonic delight in what the critic and biographer, Cecil Lang, calls "Algernonic exaggeration": When people began to talk scathingly about his homosexuality and other sexual proclivities, he circulated a story that he had engaged in pederasty and bestiality with a monkey — and then eaten it. How many of the stories were true and how many invented is unclear. Oscar Wilde called him "a braggart in matters of vice, who had done everything he could to convince his fellow citizens of his homosexuality and bestiality without being in the slightest degree a homosexual or a bestialiser."

In December 1862, Swinburne accompanied Scott and his guests on a trip to Tynemouth. Scott writes in his memoirs that, as they walked by the sea, Swinburne declaimed the as yet unpublished 'Hymn to Proserpine' and 'Laus Veneris' in his lilting intonation, while the waves 'were running the whole length of the long level sands towards Cullercoats and sounding like far-off acclamations'.

Swinburne possessed a curious combination of frail health and strength. He was small and slightly built, but an excellent swimmer and the first to climb Culver Cliff on the Isle of Wight. He had an extremely excitable disposition: people who met him described him as a "demoniac boy" who would go skipping about the room declaiming poetry at the top of his voice. In this as in many things, moderation was not the standard for him. Excess was. Once or twice he had fits, thought to be epileptic, in public; but he made this condition much worse by drinking past excess to unconsciousness. More than once he was delivered to the door in the small of the night, dead drunk. Throughout the 1860s and '70s he rode an alcoholic cycle of dissolution, collapse, drying out at home in the country, then returning to London where he would begin the cycle all over again.

His mania for masochism, particularly flagellation, most probably started in early childhood at Eton and was encouraged by his later friendships with Richard Monckton Milnes (one of Tennyson's fellow Apostles), who introduced him to the works of the Marquis de Sade, and Richard Burton, the Victorian explorer and adventurer. Swinburne was an alcoholic and algolagniac (a desire for sexual gratification through inflicting pain on oneself or others; sadomasochism). He found life difficult, unfulfilling but still his poetic talents pushed to the fore.

Although Swinburne continued to publish some works in periodicals in 1865 he was granted recognition by both public and critics with Atalanta in Calydon written in the style of a classical Greek tragedy.

There followed "Laus Veneris" and Poems and Ballads (1866), with their sexually charged passages, absolutely decadent for polite Victorian society, which were attacked all the more violently as a result. The poems written in homage of Sappho of Lesbos such as "Anactoria" and "Sapphics" were especially savaged. The volume also contained poems such as "The Leper," "Laus Veneris," and "St Dorothy" which evoke both Swinburne's and a general Victorian fascination with the Middle Ages, and are explicitly mediaeval in style, tone and construction. With its publication came instant notoriety. He was now identified with indecent and decadent themes and the precept of art for art's sake.

Swinburne's meeting in 1867 with his long-time hero Mazzini, the Italian patriot living in England in exile, was the beginning of a poetical journey that now became more serious and more engaged with serious thought, initially leading to the political poems in the volume Songs Before Sunrise.

Also in 1867 he was introduced to Adah Isaacs Menken, the American actress, poet and circus rider, whose main fame seemed to be riding naked on a horse (in fact she wore tight nude coloured clothing) for her performance in the melodrama Mazeppa (itself based on a poem by Lord Byron). Although they had a short affair Adah's quote implies that Swinburne was not ready for a relationship that did not involve some self-sabotage; "I can't make him understand that biting's no use."

In 1879, with Swinburne nearly dead from alcoholism and dissolution, his legal advisor Theodore Watts-Dunton took him in, and was gradually successful in getting him to adapt to a healthier lifestyle. Swinburne lived the rest of his life at Watts-Dunton's house. He saw less and less of his old bohemian friends, who thought him a prisoner at The Pines, but his growing deafness also accounts for some of his decreased sociability. By now Swinburne was 42, and was moving from a young man of rebelliousness to a figure of social respectability. It was said of Watts-Dunton that he saved the man and killed the poet.

It is clear that Swinburne had an addictive personality, and clearly incapable of moderation in his pursuit of any chosen vices. This, of course, would both nourish and perhaps sabotage his poetic career. His poetry follows the somewhat clichéd pattern of early flourish and later decline; indeed some of the fresher pieces in the second and third series of Poems and Ballads (published in 1878 and 1889) were actually written during his days at Oxford. Nevertheless, his last collection, A Channel Passage, has some beautiful poems, including "The Lake of Gaube."

He is best remembered as the supreme technician in metre, with a versatility which exceeds even Tennyson's, but which lacks a corresponding emotional range. His obsessions are not widely enough shared; and if he cannot shock us by the strangeness of his desires nor the shrillness of his anti-theistical exclamations, often what remains is not enough to fully engage with the audience.

Swinburne is considered a poet of the decadent school, although he perhaps professed to more vice than he actually indulged in to advertise his deviance. Common gossip of the time reported that he also had a deep crush on the explorer Sir Richard Francis Burton, despite the fact that Swinburne himself abhorred travel. Fact and fiction are easily absorbed by the other so are difficult to untangle even now.

Many critics consider his mastery of vocabulary, rhyme and metre impressive, although he has also been criticised for his florid style and word choices that only fit the rhyme scheme rather than contributing to the meaning of the piece. A. E. Housman, although a critic, had great praise for his rhyming ability: to Swinburne the sonnet was child's play: the task of providing four rhymes was not hard enough, and he wrote long poems in which each stanza required eight or ten rhymes, and wrote them so that he never seemed to be saying anything for the rhyme's sake.

Throughout his career Swinburne published literary criticism of great worth. His deep knowledge of world literatures contributed to a critical style rich in quotation, allusion, and comparison. He is particularly noted for discerning studies of Elizabethan dramatists and of many English and French poets and novelists. As well he was a noted essayist and wrote two novels.

Swinburne was nominated for the Nobel Prize in Literature every year from 1903 to 1907 and then again in 1909.

H.P. Lovecraft, the master of the dark side and a decent poet himself, considered Swinburne "the only real poet in either England or America after the death of Mr. Edgar Allan Poe."

Swinburne was also responsible for devising a poetic form called the roundel, a variation of the French Rondeau form. In 1883 he published A Century of Roundels with several of the roundels dedicated to Dante's sister, the poet Christina Georgina Rossetti. Swinburne wrote to Edward Burne-Jones in 1883: "I have got a tiny new book of songs or songlets, in one form and all manner of metres ... just coming out, of which Miss Rossetti has accepted the dedication. I hope you and Georgie [his wife Georgiana] will find something to like among a hundred poems of nine lines each, twenty-four of which are about babies or small children".

Opinions of the Roundel poems move between those who find them captivating and brilliant, to others who find them merely clever and contrived. One of them, A Baby's Death, was set to music by the English composer Sir Edward Elgar as the song "Roundel: The little eyes that never knew Light".

After the first Poems and Ballads, Swinburne's later poetry was devoted more to philosophy and politics, including the unification of Italy, particularly in the volume Songs before Sunrise. He did not stop writing love poetry entirely, indeed it was only in 1882 that his great epic-length poem, Tristram of Lyonesse, was published, its contents lyrical rather than shocking. His versification, and especially his rhyming technique, remain of high quality to the end.

Algernon Charles Swinburne died of influenza, at the Pines in London on April 10th, 1909 at the age of 72. He was buried at St. Boniface Church, Bonchurch on the Isle of Wight.

Algernon Charles Swinburne – A Concise Bibliography

Verse Drama
The Queen Mother (1860)
Rosamond (1860)
Chastelard (1865)
Bothwell (1874)
Mary Stuart (1881)
Marino Faliero (1885)
Locrine (1887)
The Sisters (1892)
Rosamund, Queen of the Lombards (1899)

Poetry
Atalanta in Calydon (1865)*
Poems and Ballads (1866)
Songs Before Sunrise (1871)
Songs of Two Nations (1875)
Erechtheus (1876)*
Poems and Ballads, Second Series (1878)
Songs of the Springtides (1880)
Studies in Song (1880)
The Heptalogia, or the Seven against Sense. A Cap with Seven Bells (1880)
Tristram of Lyonesse (1882)
A Dark Month & Other Poems
A Century of Roundels (1883)
A Midsummer Holiday and Other Poems (1884)
Poems and Ballads, Third Series (1889)
Astrophel and Other Poems (1894)
The Tale of Balen (1896)
A Channel Passage and Other Poems (1904)

*Although formally tragedies, Atalanta in Calydon and Erechtheus are traditionally included with his poetry.

Criticism
William Blake: A Critical Essay (1868, new edition 1906)
Under the Microscope (1872)
George Chapman: A Critical Essay (1875)
Essays and Studies (1875)
A Note on Charlotte Brontë (1877)
A Study of Shakespeare (1880)
A Study of Victor Hugo (1886)
A Study of Ben Johnson (1889)
Studies in Prose and Poetry (1894)

The Age of Shakespeare (1908)
Shakespeare (1909)

Major Collections
The Poems of Algernon Charles Swinburne, 6 vols. 1904.
The Tragedies of Algernon Charles Swinburne, 5 vols. 1905.
The Complete Works of Algernon Charles Swinburne, 20 vols. Bonchurch Edition. 1925-7.
The Swinburne Letters, 6 vols. 1959-62.

www.ingramcontent.com/pod-product-compliance
Lightning Source LLC
Chambersburg PA
CBHW060100050426
42448CB00011B/2552